a youth devotional on friendship

my own monster

a youth devotional on friendship

my Own monster

Jeff & Ramona Tucker

foreword by Katy Hudson

SHAW BOOKS
an imprint of WATERBROOK PRESS

My Own Monster

A SHAW BOOK

PUBLISHED BY WATERBROOK PRESS

2375 Telstar Drive, Suite 160

Colorado Springs, Colorado 80920

A division of Random House, Inc.

ISBN 0-87788-583-4

A different version of this work was previously published under the title *Maximum Friendship.*

Printed in the United States of America

2001

10 9 8 7 6 5 4 3 2 1

For Albert and Josie Cramer,

who lovingly give us the best gift of all— their friendship.

A special thanks to Evangeline and Brian,

who've shown us that family can be best friends;

Jack, Corinne, and Charlene for their creative brainstorming;

and the HFC youth group for their good-natured role

in being guinea pigs for this book!

contents

My Own Monster

I turn my head, there's nothing there
All I own is my thoughts for my fears
I close the door to keep out the bad
I plug my ears to keep out these fears
And I cry

So hold me close, for I'm so tired of holding myself...

They say there's a place that I can hide
In the shadow of Your wings
Oh Lord, bring me to this place of refuge
No more tears

So hold me close, for I'm so tired of holding myself...

—KATY HUDSON

Before I sing "My Own Monster" on stage, I like to ask the kids in the audience if they still have night-lights in their bedrooms. You wouldn't believe how loud the cheer is that comes back every time. Then I expose one of my more personal secrets—that I, too, struggle with fear. Before I realized how many kids my age are afraid to be alone at night, I thought I was one of a few who had major head problems. Now I know differently.

I was in my room one day, just singing and writing, when the idea for "My Own Monster" came to me. The song didn't have an amazing background to it, like I saw a ghost or a demon. Instead, God showed me my fear. I don't know if I can adequately describe this experience; it was something very personal to me. For a little while, I felt like I was living a scary movie. But I knew in the end that everything was going to be okay. I had to write this song because when I sing, I can say all the things I don't want to speak. It's my way of talking about things. And I want others to know they are not alone when they, like me, struggle with sleeping and fear.

While writing the chorus, I came to the realization that I had been avoiding my problem, sometimes by doing little things like covering my head with my pillow or having night-lights on. And when those strategies were getting me nowhere, I would basically try to hold myself through the night. Then there was that one night when it all came clear. I needed God to help me, to hold me. My parents had advised me that whenever I was scared, I should pray to God and tell the devil to flee. I started remembering all that, and it helped me get through the night. It showed me that God really is the only one who can take away the fear.

The song deals with fear but also with the fact that you can't give in to fear—if you do, it'll eat you up. I know lots of people deal with fear, not only at night but also in relationships; sometimes friendships can seem dark and uncertain. There is a refuge for your mind, as this song says. God is our refuge. We are safe underneath his wings.

I believe God uses songs and journals and devotions to help us deal with the problems in our lives. The devotions in this book won't answer all of your questions about life or fear or friendship (there are so many!), but they *will* help you grow closer to Christ. They will open your eyes to the freedom God has in store for you. Maybe twelve years down the line, when we are all a bit older, you will pick up this book and dust it off and realize how God used it in the process of shaping your friendships and making you into the man or woman you will have become by then.

It's no coincidence that you picked up this book. All things happen for a reason. So keep it real…and read on!

—KATY HUDSON

the importance of friends

When we asked the teens in our youth group to write down the three things that were most important to them, two tied for first place: "friends" and "family." "School or peer pressure," which also has to do with friendship, took third place!

Being a teen isn't easy. You're faced with more concerns than ever before: peer pressure, self-esteem, romance, family problems, questions about whether God is really there or not. Maybe you're confused about who you are and how you fit into this crazy, topsy-turvy world. Or perhaps you're lonely. You might have lots of "friends," but you still feel like you're in a locker all by yourself and someone has slammed the door.

Together we'll look at different types of friendship to discover tips for making the good ones last and for breaking off the not-so-good ones. And as we share the stories of the kids in this book, you'll find help for areas you're struggling with. Things like how to handle annoying siblings and snobbish cliques, how to forgive friends when they drop you, and how to resolve sticky conflicts.

In these pages you'll find questions that will make you think, space to write down your responses, friendly suggestions for activities, and things to think or pray about during the rest of the day. Nothing would make us happier than to see this book well worn and crowded with your scribbles, thoughts, and discoveries.

But overall, we pray that you'll discover—in this book and in the pages of Scripture—a Friend who's got all the number-one qualities you could ever want or need. We'll let you fill in the name!

friendship power

Romans 12:4-6

Amanda was exasperated. She and Christopher were at it again. She felt like throwing him and all his stubborn ideas right out the window. Friends were supposed to stick together, right? And think and act like twins?

Amanda and Christopher had been good friends for two years; they'd been drawn together like magnets. But lately she and Christopher always rubbed each other the wrong way.

Amanda's family was conservative. She couldn't listen to anything but the mellowest Christian music, and her curfew was at ten every night, even on weekends.

Christopher was almost exactly her opposite. His CD collection was mostly Christian rock, and his parents didn't even set a curfew. They said they trusted him to make his own wise decisions.

Amanda and Christopher were always knocking heads over that one, wondering, "So, who's right anyway?" They disagreed on a lot of other issues, too.

Do Opposites Really Attract?

Friendship isn't automatic. You don't just push a button on a machine and—*ka-chink!*—out falls a perfect, made-to-order friend. Actually, that would be pretty boring. You don't need a duplicate copy of yourself as a friend—it would be like staring at yourself every day.

Friendship doesn't always mean agreeing. Differences can be good. They make us think and help us grow as individuals. And they make us stronger because we have to make our own decisions.

Good friends learn to compromise and to give each other freedom to be who they are. They are dedicated to each other and to learning how to make their relationship work. Good friends let each other be unique, and they challenge each other to become the absolute best they can be.

Unlikely People

Some of the most unlikely people in the Bible were friends. Take Moses and Aaron, for example. Moses was a terrific organizer; God needed his talent when the Israelites were wandering in the desert. But Moses had a problem. He couldn't speak well—he'd get so nervous that he'd stutter and stumble over his words. He needed his brother, Aaron, who was a great speaker but tended to go off the deep end when Moses wasn't around. (When Moses trekked up the mountain to get the Ten Commandments, Aaron allowed the people to stumble in a major way—they built a golden calf to worship instead of God.)

The book of Exodus tells the story. Together, Moses and Aaron were unstoppable. And what's more, they were brothers! That's a pretty good example of what working together can do.

Two other friends who worked together at a task were Elijah and Elisha. A poor guy, Elijah was always running around the country without a roof over his head. Elisha, on the other hand, had five oxen. In Bible times that meant he was a lot better off. Today it would be like Elijah having a junker of a car while Elisha had a Porsche Boxster. If you want to read their story, check out 2 Kings 2.

Even though they were about as far apart in social position and money as you could get, they still became close friends. They realized that differences were necessary and normal and that each one of them still had a special place in God's plan.

Paul explained it in Romans 12:4-6:

> Just as each of us has one body with many members,
> and these members do not all have the same function,
> so in Christ we who are many form one body, and each
> member belongs to all the others. We have different
> gifts, according to the grace given us.

Like and Unlike

Evaluate your two closest friends. How are they like you?

How are they different from you?

Thank God today for giving you unique friends and for giving you such a special place in his plans.

through thick and thin

Romans 12:10-13

Dad was on the warpath again. In fact, he seemed to be yelling even more than usual—which was most of the time.

Jennifer sighed. She and Dad could never agree on anything. Lately Jennifer had worked especially hard to keep her room clean and to help around the house, but he didn't seem to notice. Even when she did something extra, like washing his car, Dad always found something wrong with it.

She felt like she couldn't even talk to her dad anymore. Whenever he came home—*if* he came home—he was drunk. And then, when he got home, he'd have a drink in his hand within five minutes. She was tired of hearing her parents fight. They even fought when her friends came over. It was so embarrassing that she didn't ask anyone to come over anymore.

Except Kristen. Kristen was her always-there friend. They did everything together—worked at Burger King after school on Mondays and Wednesdays, sang in the choir on Sundays, and went out together on weekends. They shared everything, down to Diet Cokes and pocket change.

When Jennifer's dad yelled, Kristen didn't get embarrassed like

Jennifer's other friends did. She just rolled her eyes and smiled that twinkly smile that made Jennifer immediately feel better. Kristen understood and loved her just the same, alcoholic dad and all.

Jennifer trusted Kristen completely. Kristen would do anything for her—she was that kind of friend.

A Loyal Friend

Kristen was a loyal friend both in time and heart. It didn't matter to her one bit that Jennifer had a rough home life. She just took it in stride and went right on being a true friend.

David and Jonathan had a loyal friendship like that. Even though they lived a long time ago, we can learn a lot from them. Jonathan was the son of a king, while David was only a shepherd. But that didn't stop them from being friends. Can you imagine? It's like the poorest kid in school with the rattiest clothes becoming the best friend of the richest, best-looking kid with all the name-brand clothes and a mansion of a house.

Brotherly Love

David and Jonathan had a special friendship. They grew to love each other like brothers, and they stuck together through thick and thin. You can read the story of their loyal friendship in 1 Samuel 19–20.

The Bible says this about faithful friends:

> Love each other with genuine affection, and take
> delight in honoring each other. Never be lazy in your
> work, but serve the Lord enthusiastically.

Be glad for all God is planning for you. Be patient in trouble, and always be prayerful. When God's children are in need, be the one to help them out. (Romans 12:10-13, NLT)

Young Faithful

 Do you have a special friend you can always count on? Why do you feel that way?

Ask God to help you be a more faithful friend this week, and think of some ways you can show your friends that you are loyal to them.

even when the truth hurts

Ecclesiastes 4:9-10,12

"I can't believe it!" Travis muttered to himself as he threw himself onto his unmade bed. "Kyle is supposed to be a Christian."

Travis was ticked off. He had thought Kyle was a cool guy. He didn't wear the words SUPER CHRISTIAN plastered in capital letters across his chest or anything like that, but he was pretty cool—at least most of the time.

But lately things had changed. Travis's group of friends no longer seemed good enough for Kyle. And today at school he'd heard that Kyle had taken the drug ecstasy at a party last weekend.

What good is all this stuff he told me about Christ anyway? It doesn't seem to make any difference to him now, Travis thought. He felt like calling Kyle. After all, they *had* been good friends. And shouldn't friends be honest with each other?

He reached for the phone. But then Travis wondered, *What if he gets mad when I ask him what he's up to? Or worse, what if he laughs at me?* Slamming down the phone, Travis dropped his chin into his hands. *I'm such a chicken.*

A Shot in the Arm

Kyle isn't the only one who needs a good buddy to turn him around. We all need it sometimes. Maybe we aren't doing something radical like taking drugs, but there are other things—like gossiping, having a bad attitude, or ignoring the new kid.

In Isaiah 38–39 we read a story about two friends: Isaiah the prophet and Hezekiah the king. Hezekiah was a good guy, but he was also human. He made a big mistake. When the king of Babylon sent him a get-well present, it went to his head. He was so pleased about it that he showed the Babylonians (his country's enemies) where all his gold and silver and other treasures were. It was like showing a robber where you keep your money stashed.

Hezekiah didn't think past his own emotions to what he was doing to his kingdom and the people. When Isaiah heard about it, he marched directly to the king and confronted him, telling Hezekiah that, because of what he had done, the Babylonians would invade the country and carry its people and treasures into captivity.

It Takes Guts

Isaiah was one gutsy dude. Even though the king could have anyone executed that he wanted to, Isaiah wasn't afraid. What meant more to Isaiah was keeping a covenant (agreement) of honesty with his friend, even when his friend got off on the wrong track.

Most likely, none of your friends would have you executed—even if they got mad enough! But they might blow you off or go on doing what they are doing anyway. Still, God calls us to hold our friends accountable:

Two are better than one....
If one falls down,
   his friend can help him up.
But pity the man who falls
   and has no one to help him up!...
Though one may be overpowered,
   two can defend themselves.
A cord of three strands is not quickly broken.
         (Ecclesiastes 4:9-10,12)

Good Medicine

When was the last time you told a friend the truth about something good in his or her life? When was the last time you told the truth about something bad?

Good friends hold each other accountable. Make a covenant with a friend to be honest with each other—even when the truth hurts.

success—it's up to you

Hebrews 12:12-13

Amy was a cute, petite blonde and a freshman at Glendale West in Ohio. The only problem was that she had just transferred in from a school in Alabama.

Amy felt lost. Every day she dreaded going to school. The first day was the worst. Wandering down the hallways, she'd been looking for her English room. All of a sudden, a guy yelled at her, "Hey, freshman! You're not supposed to be in this hall. It's a *senior* hall. Get lost!" She'd walked away with all the dignity she could muster.

Living in the North was very different from what she was used to. Everything moved a lot faster and the kids weren't as friendly. Or maybe it just seemed that way because she didn't know anyone. She was too scared to open her mouth, because if she did, everyone would know she was different. She'd lived in Alabama all her life and she hadn't ever thought about "accents" until she moved to Ohio.

The first two months passed slowly. She still didn't have any friends. Between classes she walked alone, and she sat alone at lunch.

One Friday, after school, she rushed home and up to her room. "I hate this place! Why did Mom have to move here anyway? No one likes me!" she yelled and threw herself on her bed. Then the tears came—a whole hour of them. Her eyes looked puffy all evening.

Making Your Own Success

How do you choose your friends? Sometimes it just happens and you don't feel like you really *chose* anybody. Other times, maybe you're like Amy. You have a hard time reaching out beyond yourself even to say, "Hi, y'all!" Maybe you feel insecure and wish that someone would just say "hi" and invite you out for coffee.

Have you ever felt like Amy? If so, when?

How would you have responded to Amy if she had come to your school?

In order to have friends, you need to ask yourself, *What kind of friend do I want to be?* Friendship is more than *finding* the right person; it's also *becoming* the right person.

Essentials

If you focus on becoming loyal, trustworthy, and committed instead of groaning that you don't have friends, you might discover a few surprises. The Bible says this:

> Strengthen your feeble arms and weak knees. "Make
> level paths for your feet," so that the lame may not be
> disabled, but rather healed. (Hebrews 12:12-13)

It's up to you. You can either focus on your own loneliness or you can try to meet other people's needs. If you're concentrating on helping someone else, you won't have time to be self-conscious.

You'll find that you will start caring more about other people. And guess what? They'll begin to realize what a good friend you are. Having a committed friend is awesome!

Copy the following verse and put it in your locker, on your mirror, by your computer—someplace where you will see it every day:

> If we love each other, God lives in us, and his love has
> been brought to full expression through us....

And God himself has commanded that we must love
not only him but our Christian brothers and sisters,
too. (1 John 4:12,21, NLT)

Keep asking yourself, *What kind of friend do I want to be?* Remember,
your success story is up to you.

shy shannon

Joshua 1:5,9

It was the first day of Shannon's freshman year. She walked down the beige hallways, glancing to the left and then to the right. Her locker was here somewhere.

Where is number 292? she wondered. She found numbers 250 and 280, and then she saw them—the 290s. They were blocked by a whole bunch of laughing guys and girls.

Shannon's heart sank. Her head drooped as she hid behind her new notebook and oozed past her locker. She rounded the corner and pretended to take a long drink from the water fountain—anything to kill time.

When she walked back to her locker, no one was there. Relieved, she opened the door and hung up her jacket.

"What's my problem, anyway?" she muttered, ticked off at herself.

Then the bell rang. Oh no! She was late for class—and what was worse, on the very first day! Now she'd have to walk in and find her seat in front of everybody. Shannon felt like crawling in her locker and shutting the door—permanently.

Totally Average

Maybe you're like Shannon. You get so nervous when someone talks to you that you slam your thumb in your locker or drop your books (on the other person's feet, of course!). Or you don't feel that you're good enough to be noticed because you're not good-looking, talented, or above average in anything.

In what ways can you relate to Shannon?

Looking Beyond the Mirror

Ugh! How often have *you* looked in the mirror in the morning and winced? You check out your hair, groan, and decide it's going to be a bad hair day. Or maybe you feel like you're ugly because you have truckloads of pimples, and you don't want to be noticed until the Clearasil has done its job. You decide you may as well just give up and wear a paper bag over your head the rest of your life.

But God says that what you see on the outside is not what's most important in the long run (check out 1 Samuel 16:7 to see why). Yes, other people may look at your outside first, so you should be aware that others may judge you on your looks alone. But remember that God sees what's inside. Are you concentrating on your inside (your thoughts, emotions, attitudes) as much as on your outside?

Plucking Up Courage

After the Israelites wandered in the desert for forty years, Moses died. God appointed Joshua as the new leader and told him:

> As I was with Moses, so I will be with you; I will never leave you nor forsake you....
>
> Be strong and courageous. Do not be terrified; do not be discouraged, for the LORD your God will be with you wherever you go. (Joshua 1:5,9)

If God could do that for Joshua, who was in charge of thousands of people, he can do it for you, too! The next time you feel like dog food (and maybe think you look like it), reread that verse.

 Do you know anyone like Shy Shannon? (Maybe it's you.) Make some notes about what you could say to him or her this week.

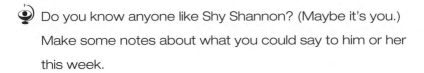

Write out Joshua 1:5,9 so you can carry it with you. Or use it to encourage a friend!

toss-aside tim

Philippians 2:3-4

"Hey, Tim!" Jerry's voice boomed across the parking lot. "How was your date with Kelly last night?"

"Terrific!" Tim grinned, showing perfect white teeth. "She's a great girl." As he slicked his brown hair back, it fell perfectly into place.

All the girls thought Tim was Hunk of the Year. Always perfectly dressed in the right clothes, he was the biggest stud of Fremont High. And he knew it.

"Are you going out with her again?" Jerry asked.

"Naw. She's okay and everything, but she's really not my type." And Tim went on to explain for five minutes why she wasn't.

Tim treated everyone alike—it didn't matter whether they were guys or girls. He was a be-a-friend-once-and-then-toss-you-aside kind of guy. Why shouldn't he be that way? Tim figured he had his pick of anyone he wanted to be friends with. They were all at his feet, begging to be his friends because he was such a cool guy and all.

Jerry shook his head. He just couldn't understand Tim.

Straight to the Head

Perfect Tim. He was a popular guy. The only problem was that he let it go straight to his head. Ever heard the saying "His head's so fat that he couldn't get it through the doorway"? Well, Tim's was so big that it could have taken over the world—or at least his world, Fremont High.

Right now it's cool to be like Tim. But sooner or later, Tim's going to fall over his own feet and—*splat!*—there goes the reputation. Suddenly he won't seem so handsome anymore. You can't toss people aside or treat them like objects for long. Soon they won't want to be around you.

Attitude Check

In Philippians 2:3-4 Paul said,

> Do nothing out of selfish ambition or vain conceit, but
> in humility consider others better than yourselves. Each
> of you should look not only to your own interests, but
> also to the interests of others.

 Evaluate yourself honestly. How do you treat other kids at school?

Write down examples of how you'd like to change.

Ask God to help you treat others the way you want to be treated.

merry mary?

Galatians 6:9-10

"Good morning, Ashley! Isn't it just a be-e-eautiful day? I love spring, don't you?" Mary gushed as she came into Ashley's room.

Ashley groaned as she turned over in bed. Every morning it was the same scene. She felt like ducking back under her covers and hiding. Since Mary was also an eighth grader and lived on her block, she had taken it upon herself to meet Ashley at her house so they could walk to school together every day.

Go away! Ashley exclaimed inside.

Mary bubbled, "I just couldn't wait to get up today so I could wear my new jeans to school. The girls are going to love them, don't you think?"

Ashley propped open one of her blue eyes—just a corner, though. Enough to see Mary perched on the edge of her bed, looking 110 percent awake and ready to go, as usual.

Ashley sighed and dragged herself up in a fog while Mary chattered on happily. *She can't be this happy all the time! It's impossible!* Ashley thought. Ashley groaned again as she pulled on her jeans and a rumpled T-shirt.

Bursting the Bubble

We all know someone like Merry Mary. Maybe it's the girl at school who is always so irritatingly bubbly—*nobody* could be that happy all the time. Or maybe it's the guy who's the clown of the class, who laughs even when other kids give him a hard time.

Merry Mary may have always seemed happy on the outside, but what was happening on the inside? What Ashley didn't know was that Mary's parents were breaking up. They fought every night, and it echoed in Mary's brain. Scared they'd get a divorce and yet wanting the screaming to end, Mary felt caught—and guilty. She wondered if it was her fault.

The up-front happy stuff was just a big fake. Too embarrassed to tell anyone what was going on at home, Mary hid her problems.

Real People

No matter how people act, you have to look beyond their words and actions to what they're *really* thinking and feeling. Maybe they need you to ask, "How are you *really* doing?" and to take time for them. They need you to show that you care about them and are interested in them personally.

In Galatians, Paul encouraged us to keep doing good to others:

> Let us not become weary in doing good, for at the
> proper time we will reap a harvest if we do not give up.
> Therefore, as we have opportunity, let us do good to all
> people, especially to those who belong to the family of
> believers. (6:9-10)

If someone you know is happy, it doesn't always mean that he or she has personal problems. But be sensitive. You might be surprised what you find out when you keep your eyes and ears open.

The Great Pretenders

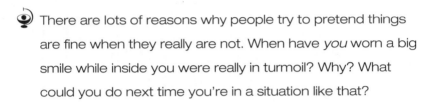 There are lots of reasons why people try to pretend things are fine when they really are not. When have *you* worn a big smile while inside you were really in turmoil? Why? What could you do next time you're in a situation like that?

How can you become the kind of person in whom others will confide, not feeling that they have to pretend around you?

Ask Jesus to give you a new, special love for the Merry Marys in your life.

one-track ted

1 John 3:18

Ted was Mr. Average in just about everything. But he could be considered almost handsome—until he opened his mouth, that is. Then he bored everyone to death.

Ted was at it again. Andrea could tell he was interested in her, and she sort of liked him. So she had invited him over to her house yesterday after school. He'd even offered to carry her books. She couldn't believe it! He was so-o-o nice.

Then he blew it. Big time. When they climbed Andrea's front porch steps, they'd run into her older brother Brian. Both Brian and Ted were into cars. And not just into them—they breathed, ate, and slept cars. Talking about engines to them was like eating chocolate chip cookies to Andrea. They had spent an hour talking about turbochargers and dual exhausts, and finally they took off to see the car Brian was overhauling in the garage, leaving Andrea slumped and bored on the porch.

She hadn't even seen Ted the rest of the evening. He'd waved good-bye and yelled happily, "Hey, thanks for inviting me!"

Today, Ted was at her locker again. "Andrea, your brother is terrific! And he knows so much." Ted launched off into lingo about boosting horsepower again. Andrea felt like screaming.

One-Track Minds

Everyone knows a one-focused guy or girl. Maybe like Ted, the car expert, he talks about cars every time one rolls by. When you try to switch the subject, he looks at you blankly like you don't exist. Maybe it's Laura, whose mind holds only visions of the nearest shopping mall. Or Bob, the Bible banger, whose Bible is so big he can't even stuff it in his locker.

When these people are around, you might feel pretty angry. They always seem to crank their mouths in gear, but rarely their ears.

Switching Tracks

What words do you think describe one-track people? Maybe *selfish, insensitive.* But have you ever thought that maybe they just don't know what else to talk about? They feel insecure, so they pick the one subject that they know more about than anyone else. Or they could be genuinely interested in a certain subject and honestly don't know they're boring you to death.

But you know what? If you really listen and show interest, you might learn something. Even better, they might realize they have a genuine friend in you and start listening to what *you* have to say.

The Bible encourages us to put guts behind what we say and do:

> Dear children, let us not love with words or tongue but with actions and in truth. (1 John 3:18)

How About You?

🌐 Are you like Ted, wanting to talk only about the things you're interested in? Do you get bored easily? Make notes here about your last two conversations today. (If you can't remember them, maybe that's a clue about your listening powers!)

🌐 How can you show someone you're really listening to him or her? How can this be part of loving "with actions and in truth"?

This week, when someone is boring you, turn your ears on. You might learn something about that person—or even yourself! Ask God to make you a more sensitive listener.

can't-make-up-my-mind carol

Philippians 1:9-10; 2:2

"Hey, Carol! Are you going to Shelly's party Friday?" wheezed Jackie, a little out of breath from her dash down the school halls. Jackie never walked; she always took off like she'd seen the biggest, hairiest spider that ever crawled.

"*Everybody's* going! Susan, Eric, and...," Jackie chattered on. Everyone who was *anyone,* she meant. There were about ten kids in Carol and Jackie's group who hung out together.

"Are you going, Jackie?" Carol asked quietly.

"You bet! It's gonna be great."

"Well, if you're going, I guess I'll go," Carol said slowly.

"Great! See you later!" Jackie called and tore down the hall.

Carol bumped into Cyndi on the way to her bicycle. "Want to grab a Coke, Carol?" Cyndi asked, flipping her blonde hair back. "I'm meeting the others there."

"I guess I'll go, if you're going," Carol hesitated.

Rather exasperated, Cyndi drawled, "Well, come on, let's get going. We're already late."

All the girls knew Carol couldn't make up her mind about anything, whether it was choosing what video to watch or where to eat or even what to wear. That was just Carol. It always had been and probably always would be. Her friends had gotten used to it.

Wishy-Washy People

How many people do you know who are like Carol? People who can't ever seem to make up their minds are usually insecure—they so want to be a part of a group that they're afraid of making a decision that's different from everyone else's. Fitting into a particular group is more important to them than being who they really are.

Carol had a hard time standing up for anything. She was a major pushover, and everyone knew it. But there's more about Carol. The sad thing is, she can't even stand up for what she believes in. Things like dating standards and beliefs about God. Whether she acts like a Christian or not depends on who she's with.

Stand-Up Power

The Bible says this about wishy-washy people:

> A doubtful mind is as unsettled as a wave of the sea
> that is driven and tossed by the wind. People like that
> should not expect to receive anything from the Lord.
> They can't make up their minds. They waver back and
> forth in everything they do. (James 1:6-8, NLT)

And Revelation 3:15-16 says this:

> I know your deeds, that you are neither cold nor hot. I
> wish you were either one or the other! So, because you
> are lukewarm—neither hot nor cold—I am about to
> spit you out of my mouth.

God wants us to learn to take a stand, whether it is easy or not. Making decisions is part of the growing-up process.

Firm Ground

Have you ever been wishy-washy on a decision? If so, when? What was the result?

What could you do the next time you're struggling with wishy-washiness?

If you have a hard time making up your mind on things, remember what Paul said in Philippians:

> This is my prayer: that your love may abound more
> and more in knowledge and depth of insight, so that
> you may be able to discern what is best and may be
> pure and blameless until the day of Christ....
> Make my joy complete by being like-minded,
> having the same love, being one in spirit and purpose.
> (1:9-10; 2:2)

Copy these verses into a notebook or post them on your bathroom mirror so you'll always have them when you need them. In your prayer time today, ask God to help you stand firm.

who put on these price tags, anyway?

Jeremiah 1:5

William slammed the padlock on his athletic locker. *I'm such a clod!* he thought. *How come I have to be so uncoordinated?* He picked at the worn leather on his football. He felt pretty lucky just to have made it onto the junior varsity team this year.

William felt like he was constantly messing up. And that everyone saw him trip over his size 13 feet at least once a day. Like a giant Labrador retriever, he galloped through the school halls. He never could get his arms and legs to go in the same direction at the same time. And besides that, he had braces—a full set of gleaming metal that knocked your eyeballs out when he smiled.

I wish I were like Ron. He always has it together—and he's even got muscles in all the right places! William kicked his locker for the third time that day.

The "I Wish" Syndrome

Have you ever wished you looked like someone else? Or even *were* someone else? Maybe you've battled with being chunky your whole life—you just *look* at a Hershey's candy bar and it melts right onto your hips. Maybe you're in high school now, but you still weigh only eighty-nine pounds—same as you did in sixth grade—and the only position you could play on the football team is the football. Or maybe your parents are divorced, and you wish you had perfect parents like your friends do.

One of a Kind

There are lots of reasons why you might wish you were someone else. But you know what? God created you as a unique individual. It's like what he said to the prophet Jeremiah:

> Before I formed you in the womb I knew you,
>> before you were born I set you apart. (Jeremiah 1:5)

God knew you even while you were being created! And he made you as you are—a redhead, an athlete, a good cook, whatever. He gave you naturally wavy or straight hair. And by putting together millions of variations, he made you—and there's no one else exactly like you in the whole world!

God values your uniqueness. And because he has created you as you are, he expects you to use what he's given you. Maybe you aren't the greatest athlete in the world, but you can bake up a storm. Then bake brownies for someone who is down. Maybe you're not a mechanical genius on cars like your buddy, but you are great with math. Then tutor someone who's really struggling in math.

Don't slip into the common trap of determining your self-worth by outward things like grades or good looks. We're created in the image of

God (see Ephesians 2:10), so we already have worth. Like William, we need to take our eyes off ourselves. We need to stop asking ourselves, *How do I look? How am I doing?* And we need to start helping someone else.

Through Your Own Eyes

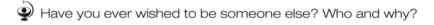 Have you ever wished to be someone else? Who and why?

 List some things you're good at.

How can you use these talents you've just listed to help others?

The next time you wish you were someone else, refer back to your list of talents. Thank God that he made you as a unique individual!

who's your hero?

Ephesians 5:1-4,8,15-16

Jessica and J. D. bounced up and down in their seats. They couldn't wait for the concert to start. After saving up for the tickets, they knew it would be worth it. And they'd even talked Mom and Dad into letting them go— a major miracle.

It was almost eight o'clock. Soon she'd come on. They couldn't believe they were actually going to see her after listening to her CDs for two years. And this year she'd been in the top ten almost every week.

But after the concert, J. D.'s and Jessica's steps slowed as they walked home. They were both disappointed—maybe she wasn't all they'd built her up to be. The concert was pretty good but not what they had expected. She sang only two of her hit songs, and the rest must have been old stuff they didn't know.

Hero Worship

All of us have heroes. When we were kids, it might have been our father or mother or the ice cream man who drove the truck with the jingly bells.

Maybe now it's a rock or movie star. It could be your favorite macho lawyer on TV or the girl on the commercials with the perfect body.

But whoever your hero is, you need to measure that person by this passage of Scripture:

> Be imitators of God…as dearly loved children and live a life of love.…
>
> But among you there must not be even a hint of sexual immorality, or of any kind of impurity, or of greed.… Nor should there be obscenity, foolish talk or coarse joking, which are out of place, but rather thanksgiving.…
>
> For you were once darkness, but now you are light in the Lord.…
>
> Be very careful, then, how you live—not as unwise but as wise, making the most of every opportunity, because the days are evil. (Ephesians 5:1-4,8,15-16)

Not All They're Cracked Up to Be

Human heroes usually aren't all we think they are. And sometimes we're disappointed like J. D. and Jessica were. When that happens, the hero takes a rather nasty fall off your pedestal. Usually it's pretty hard for him to get back on. Even if he does manage it, now you see the cracks where you had to glue him back together.

Maybe this has happened in your own family. You've found out that Dad—who you thought was perfect—has been having an affair. Or Mom, the always happy and stable woman, had to take off work for a month because of mental depression. Or maybe you discovered that your adored older brother is gay. You're confused.

There is only one real hero. This hero never falls off his pedestal, because he can't sin—it's not a part of his nature. He is always perfect. Who's the real hero? Jesus Christ, the only one who will never fail or disappoint us. And even better, he's approachable—at any time, at all times. You don't even have to buy tickets to see him!

On the Pedestal

List two people who influence your decisions the most. In light of God's standards in Ephesians 5, are they a positive or negative influence on you? Give specifics.

Ask God to give you *his* wisdom about who you put on your pedestal.

the lone ranger

Matthew 7:1-2

Jack the Jock strutted down the hall of Lincoln High. His classmates turned from their chatter to watch him. Last night, as usual, he had wowed them all at the soccer game by scoring a hat trick (three goals) in a tough game against Westmont. The guy was incredible—"Super Stuff," they called him. He was good at anything and everything athletic.

He was such a together guy. He did everything well, and what's more, he did it by himself. His grades topped the chart. And because he was such an awesome guy, the other kids didn't even get mad when he wrecked the grading curve.

But for some reason Jack steered clear of his classmates. It wasn't that Jack was mean or sulky or anything like that; he just didn't hang around with them, and they couldn't figure out why. Then after a while, they convinced themselves, "Well, he doesn't need us. He's got everything he needs."

Meanwhile, Jack padded down the halls to class alone.

On the Outside

On the outside, Jack seemed totally independent. But what was he like on the inside?

What nobody knew was that Jack stayed aloof on purpose. He wanted friends, but he was scared for anyone to get to know him too well. Because his dad had divorced his mom, he felt that he had to be the man of the house now. Two years after the divorce, his mom still acted like a basket case and threatened to kill herself when she got depressed. And what's worse, both of his parents were supposed to be Christians.

At the Heart

All of us know people who are loners. Usually we label them—"He's a nerd"; "She's so stuck-up"; "He's a jock"—because that way we can box them up neatly. It's easy to attach stereotypes to people because of their age, social rank, or sex. How many times have you heard generalizations like "All teenagers are irresponsible!" "Dumb blonde!" "Video game players are violence freaks!"? Jesus had some stern words for those who judge others:

> Do not judge, or you too will be judged. For in the
> same way you judge others, you will be judged, and
> with the measure you use, it will be measured to you.
> (Matthew 7:1-2)

In other words, if you name-call and categorize other people, the same thing will happen to you.

In Their Shoes

 Who's the lone ranger in your school? Put yourself in his or her place for a minute. How do you think that person really feels?

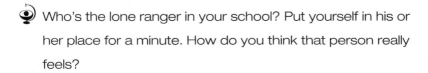

Write down one thing you can do this week for the person you listed. Then do it, knowing that God's smiling because of your actions. Ask a parent, youth leader, or close friend to keep you accountable.

the right kind of nitpicky

Proverbs 13:20

Linda's mind churned. Finally the "cool" kids had invited her to go out with them on Friday night. But there was a big problem—they were going to a park way out in the country, a place known for wild parties.

She wanted to go with them because it seemed like they had a lot of fun together. But still she felt uncomfortable. She also knew her parents wouldn't approve. So she told her new friends no. Raising their eyebrows, they said, "Hey, babe, it's your loss."

But on Monday she knew different. Shock waves radiated across the school as everyone heard about the terrible accident. Three of the kids who'd talked to her were dead. The driver had been drunk, and beer was found in the car.

The car I would have been riding in, Linda thought. Her stomach turned for the rest of the day.

Life Is a Cafeteria

Life is like going through a cafeteria line—we pick and choose the things that look good to us. One day of bad choices in food might not kill us (unless we get the stuff the cafeteria *calls* pizza), but one bad choice of a friend might. It won't necessarily kill us in body like it could have killed Linda, but it could kill us in spirit. If you choose friends who are always depressed, you could become a real bummer to be around. If you choose sarcastic friends, you might develop a sharp tongue.

Picking and Reaping

What kind of friends do you have? The Bible says you should pick your friends carefully because you'll become like them. In Proverbs, wise Solomon said,

> Whoever walks with the wise will become wise; whoever
> walks with fools will suffer harm. (13:20, NLT)

Maybe the friends you have right now won't be yours for life, but the type of friends you choose will set a pattern for the rest of your life.

Hanging Out Together

Write down the names of two of your closest friends. What kinds of reputations do they have?

Friend	Reputation

According to Proverbs 13:20, are any of your relationships harmful? What are you going to do about those that are?

Remember that the friends you choose affect who you become down the road. If God were standing next to you now, would he be pleased with the friends you hang out with? Why or why not?

Write down some qualities of people who live lives that are pleasing to God. (It might help to think of some of the godly people in the Bible.) Ask God to help you look for those qualities when you choose friends.

who's better?

James 3:16-18

Thursday night, midnight—the end of the semester. Andrew got up from his chair, stretched, and yawned. It was high-pressure time for Andrew. His brain felt like cottage cheese. He'd been studying for hours; he had to get some sleep. But first, a little more studying.

The next morning his best friend, Mark, rode up on his bike.

"I'm coming!" Andrew yelled as he grabbed his books and a bagel and barged through the door.

"Hey, dude," Mark greeted him. "Did you study for Laver's test?"

"A lot. I gotta do well on it or I don't have a chance to get into the college prep classes." Andrew sighed.

"Are you kidding?" Mark exploded. "I didn't even review the stuff. It'll be a cinch!"

Andrew couldn't believe it. Of course, Mark was a real brain and all, but not study?

As Andrew had anticipated, the test was tough. Andrew got a C minus. Guess what Mark got? He aced it.

Andrew felt sick. It was the old I'm-not-as-smart-as-him-but-I-wish-I-were problem. Why did he have to work so much harder than Mark just to pass? Suddenly, Andrew felt a cold stab of jealousy.

Pass or Fail?

There's always someone who's better than you. If you're the smartest kid in your school, then the kid from your rival school is smarter. Or maybe you're a whiz at math but impossibly dumb at English literature. Maybe you're a klutz and wish you were Joe Athletic. No matter who you are or what age you are or where you live, someone will always be better than you.

An Old Problem

King Saul had the same problem. (This story is told in 1 Samuel 18 and following chapters.) Saul was a powerful king, with all the wealth and position you could ever want. But guess who he was jealous of? A shepherd boy named David who went into battle and fought *for* Saul.

Then it got even worse. When David marched back from battle, the people sang, "Saul has slain his thousands, and David his tens of thousands" (1 Samuel 18:7). David killed at least ten times as many people as Saul. And because of jealousy, Saul tried to kill David. Why? Because on their test, David got an A and Saul got only a C minus.

You're the One Who Counts

Even though James lived a long time ago, he hit the nail on the head when he wrote about jealousy:

Where you have envy and selfish ambition, there you
find disorder and every evil practice.

But the wisdom that comes from heaven is first of all
pure; then peace-loving, considerate, submissive, full of
mercy and good fruit, impartial and sincere. Peacemak-
ers who sow in peace raise a harvest of righteousness.
(James 3:16-18)

It doesn't matter how well you do compared to someone else. What
does count is what you do and think in relation to yourself. If you try your
hardest and have a good attitude no matter what you do, then you've
passed the test with an A plus.

Name one person you're jealous of (whether it's because of
clothes, money, social status, beauty, whatever). Also, write
down why you feel jealous.

The next time you see the person you're jealous of, remind yourself that
God loves you just the way you are.

hey, did you hear about...?

Ephesians 4:29

James and Eliot each considered the other his "soul bro." Then one day James overheard Eliot talking about him in the locker room.

Two weeks ago James had finally gotten up the nerve to ask Rachel to go out with him. And she'd said yes! She was a really sweet girl, and James liked her a lot.

The way Eliot told the story, it sounded like James and Rachel had practically had sex on their date. But the truth was that nothing remotely like that had gone on.

James was disgusted—and steaming! Of course, he knew that Eliot loved to add color and details to stories, but he never thought Eliot would do something like that to him.

Standing there in his underwear, James felt more than naked. Eliot had betrayed him. He wondered what he should do about it.

James didn't have to wonder long. By the afternoon, the whole school knew "the facts" (what they thought were the facts). "Old Broadcast Mouth" Brenda, who had a megaphone for a voice, had done her job on the gossip hotline well.

The Gossip Hotline

Is all really fair in friendship and war? Or are there rules? Sometimes we wonder, especially when someone betrays us. The gossip hotline is not only news—it's *bad* news. The Bible has a lot to say about it (see Proverbs 26:17-28 for some colorful examples of how God feels about gossips).

More to the Story

Samson was a guy who felt betrayed. You see, he met this girl named Delilah—the number-one two-faced woman. Delilah was gorgeous, a real babe. Every guy was drooling over her. Well, Delilah took special interest in Samson, who was also a good-looking hunk of a guy. And he *really* liked her. A tough guy, Samson had only one weakness—pretty women. And Delilah knew it.

But there is more to the story than that. (Read about it in Judges 16.) Actually Delilah was just pretending to like Samson so she could get a secret out of him—the secret of his strength. Her persistence won out and she got what she wanted. Then she told the secret to the people who had hired her.

What was the result? Samson's long hair was chopped off, his eyes were blinded, and he was chained and tossed into prison. Eventually a building fell on him and crushed him to death.

Hopefully, a building will never fall on you! But if you are betrayed, you might feel as though one has. When someone has betrayed you, especially if you thought he or she was your friend, you just can't believe it.

One of the most powerful tools we have is the human tongue. Even though the tongue is a small part of the human body, it is extremely hard to tame (see James 3:8). What comes out of our mouth can be one of two things—encouraging or destroying. Paul gave us some guidelines:

> Do not let any unwholesome talk come out of your
> mouths, but only what is helpful for building others up
> according to their needs, that it may benefit those who
> listen. (Ephesians 4:29)

Taming the Tongue

When "Old Broadcast Mouth" Brenda tells you some sizzling news about someone in school, think about three things before you pass it on: Is it true? Is it kind? Does it have to be said?

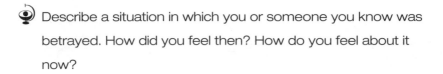 Describe a situation in which you or someone you know was betrayed. How did you feel then? How do you feel about it now?

What did you do about it? What do you think Christ would have done about it?

The next time you hear gossip, ask yourself what Jesus would do and then set the example.

superiority scene

Romans 12:16

"Best friend? Yeah, sure!" Sara muttered as Allison bounced off with the other cheerleaders in her short blue-and-white skirt. It had happened again—just like she knew it would.

Sara and Allison had been friends for so long that the other kids at school teased them about living in the same skin. But this year was different. Allison had made cheerleader and she was excited. But life had gone downhill for Sara.

Allison looked cute at the first pep rally of the year in her outfit, flinging her pompoms around. Suddenly everyone wanted Allison around. No one seemed to notice Sara, who felt like sinking right through the mint-green walls. But that wasn't too bad—she still had Allison.

By November, though, Allison didn't have time for Sara anymore. Whenever they made plans, Allison got a better offer, and off she went. She still *acted* like Sara's best friend when she had time, but Allison didn't make much time for Sara anymore. And when she did, she kept talking about what she did with the other cheerleaders and football players and how terrific it was to be part of the "cool crowd."

She thinks I'm not good enough for her anymore! Sara thought. Ooh—that hurt! *After all these years, how could she? Wasn't our friendship worth something?*

Sara felt like a worm squished on a sidewalk.

It's Your Choice

When Allison made the cheerleading squad and started meeting new people, she made a choice about how she'd treat Sara and her other old friends. But Allison got caught up in the excitement of pep rallies and games and forgot to be sensitive to Sara.

Joseph in the Old Testament also experienced some new, unexpected privileges. For one thing, he was his dad's favorite. And he wasn't very sensitive to his brothers. He strutted around in his special coat and bragged about strange dreams of superiority over them (see Genesis 37).

I'm Better than You

Later, after years of slavery and imprisonment, Joseph had another opportunity to lord it over his jealous brothers.

This time he really was high and mighty (he had become Pharaoh's number-one assistant and governor of all Egypt), but he didn't act superior to his brothers. He never once said, "I'm better than you!" Instead, he lovingly showed them that he considered them part of his "cool crowd," even after the bad things they'd done to him over the years (see Genesis 45 and 50).

Where Do You Fit in the Game?

Have you ever felt like someone was putting the superiority scene over on you? Describe the situation. How did it make you feel?

Are you lording it over anyone (it could be a next-door neighbor kid who's pesky, a new person at school, or a brother or sister)? If so, who? What can you do to change your behavior?

Tell the person you're lording it over that you've wronged him or her and that you're sorry. Ask a good friend to tell you if you're acting superior. And remember that the Bible says:

> Live in harmony with one another. Do not be proud,
> but be willing to associate with people of low position.
> Do not be conceited. (Romans 12:16)

the big letdown

Philippians 3:12-14

Kevin was sweating it out. The history final was tough—he basically had to write a survey of everything he'd learned that semester. Whew! He looked over at T. J., grinned, and gave him the thumbs-up sign. Hard study was paying off; he knew this stuff. But T. J. looked panicky.

Kevin concentrated on his test. Just as he was two-thirds through, he felt someone's eyes on him. It was T. J. He had scooted his desk over a bit and was eyeballing Kevin's answers.

Kevin couldn't believe it. His buddy T. J. was cheating—and off *his* test! Moving his arm closer to his test, Kevin blocked T. J.'s view. But then he saw T. J. mouth wordlessly, "Come on, dude!" Uncovering his test, Kevin started writing again. But his heart was heavy; he didn't even want to be T. J.'s friend anymore.

Not Perfect

Maybe, like Kevin, you've discovered that people aren't perfect. Kevin couldn't believe T. J. would cheat, especially since they were both

Christians. But even Christians aren't perfect. God calls us to be the light of the world (see Matthew 5:14), but sometimes our lights flicker. As we try to become more like Christ, we realize how tough it is to be a Christian on our own. We need Jesus—and his power—to help us.

Classic Examples

Jesus' disciples—a perfect group, right? Look again. Peter was a loud-mouthed guy who denied Christ when things got too hot for him. Thomas wouldn't believe the Lord had risen from the dead as pre-dicted —not until he saw Jesus for himself. John was a hothead, ready to call down heaven's wrath on people. The disciples were only too human, yet God used them to take big steps toward establishing his kingdom.

Paul described the goal of our lives this way:

> Not that I have…already been made perfect, but I press
> on to take hold of that for which Christ Jesus took hold
> of me. Brothers, I do not consider myself yet to have
> taken hold of it. But one thing I do: Forgetting what is
> behind and straining toward what is ahead, I press on
> toward the goal to win the prize for which God has
> called me heavenward in Christ Jesus. (Philippians
> 3:12-14)

Do you know who Paul was before he became an apostle? He was Saul, the persecutor of Christians (see Acts 9:1-19). Yet God changed his life around so that he could tell others about Jesus.

Getting Over a Letdown

🌐 Has someone ever let you down? If so, what was the situation? How did you handle it?

🌐 If the same situation happened today, how would you handle it differently?

Have *you* ever let yourself or someone else down? Whenever you feel discouraged about your failures, remember that just as God transformed the lives of his disciples, so he can change yours, too. Remember this verse in the tough times:

> You, dear children, are from God and have overcome
> [ungodly spirits], because the one who is in you is
> greater than the one who is in the world. (1 John 4:4)

enduring the dump

Psalm 34:17-19

Bianca and Stephanie were best friends. Ever since they'd both moved to the same area in fifth grade, they had been inseparable. Even their parents were friends.

One day Bianca was walking down the hall when she spied Stephanie. "Hey, Steph, want to get ice cream after school? Mom gave me some extra money."

Shock set in when Stephanie retorted, "Ice cream? Are you kidding? That's kid stuff. I'm going out with Lisa and Annette to *Denmark* Mall." She stressed "Denmark," the name of a fashionable mall on the expensive side of town.

On the way home, Bianca's pace was slower than usual. When she got to her room, she felt empty. Stephanie usually walked home with her.

The next day Bianca decided to forget it and approach Stephanie as if nothing had happened. But she didn't have the chance. Just before class started, she spied Stephanie down the hallway. As she rushed to meet her, Stephanie looked at Bianca coldly for a minute, then dismissed her with a quick wave that said, "Go away."

Shaking, Bianca backed off and made her way to the restroom before the tears started to flow. She didn't even hear the bell when it rang.

Tough Squeeze

Poor Bianca. She felt like David once felt:

> Even my best friend, the one I trusted completely,
>> the one who shared my food,
>> has turned against me. (Psalm 41:9, NLT)

Even though only one person had slam-dunked her, Bianca's world had caved in. Her heart felt like someone was squeezing the blood out of it. "I just don't understand!" she cried.

On a Deserted Island

Jesus knew what it was like to be rejected. Peter denied him three times and then ran off to save his own hide. And to top it off, most of his friends abandoned him when he was nailed to the cross. So Jesus understands when you feel as if you're on a deserted island and someone has stolen all the lifeboats.

Band-Aids

David wrote some psalms while he was running in fear for his life. He felt deserted—and betrayed—by all those he loved. And yet he had a champion Wound Healer:

The LORD hears his people when they call to him for
help.
He rescues them from all their troubles.
The LORD is close to the brokenhearted;
he rescues those who are crushed in spirit.
The righteous face many troubles,
but the LORD rescues them from each and every
one. (Psalm 34:17-19, NLT)

Has someone ever wounded or betrayed you? How did it make you feel?

Think about when you may have wounded someone else. How can the way you've felt when you were hurt or betrayed help you relate in love to the person you've hurt?

If you're wearing someone's footmark on your face today, ask Jesus to give you new hope so you can pick up and carry on.

the great blow-off

Romans 12:17-21

Guys' night out! Woo-hoo! Robert high-slapped the doorframe as he raced out the door. He'd been waiting a long time for this. A month ago, he and Jeffrey had planned to do the night up big together—just the two of them.

At 6:00, as Robert was pulling on his Levi's, Jeffrey called. "Hey, bud! Would you mind if I brought Daniel along tonight?"

Robert froze. "I thought you said it'd be the two of us."

"Yeah, I know. But I already told Daniel he could come along," Jeffrey replied.

Robert told him that he guessed it was okay and hung up. Furious, he paced in front of the mirror. *That's just great! I knew it wouldn't work out. Daniel* would *have to come tonight.*

That night, at the movies, it was so packed that they could find only two seats together. So Robert sat by himself a few rows down. Afterward, they went out for tacos. Jeffrey and Daniel were still talking about tae kwon do practice, and since Robert didn't know anything about it, he kept his mouth shut. He felt like a pesky insect hovering around the other two.

Mosquitoes Are Pests

At some time in our lives, we've all felt like pests. Whether people were actually slapping at us or not, we felt that they were.

It isn't easy when we get hyped up about something and then are disappointed. Robert felt blown off—like he wasn't important enough to be around. If Jeffrey and Daniel weren't trying to ignore him, they had a strange way of showing it.

Revenge Isn't All It's Cracked Up to Be

Getting back at them for being such snobs was the first thing on Robert's mind—a very human response. When we're hurt, we want revenge. We want to make someone else pay for hurting us. And it doesn't matter if "paying for it" is physical or emotional. The old saying "Sticks and stones may break my bones but words can never hurt me" isn't true. Verbal payback is as hurtful as physical abuse. And it happens a lot in families, even Christian ones.

Paul warned us in Romans 12:14,17-21,

> Bless those who persecute you; bless and do not
> curse.… Do not repay anyone evil for evil. Be careful to
> do what is right in the eyes of everybody. If it is pos-
> sible, as far as it depends on you, live at peace with
> everyone. Do not take revenge, my friends, but leave
> room for God's wrath, for it is written: "It is mine to
> avenge; I will repay," says the Lord. On the contrary:

"If your enemy is hungry, feed him;
   if he is thirsty, give him something to drink.
In doing this, you will heap burning coals on
      his head."

Do not be overcome by evil, but overcome evil
with good.

That's a tough scripture to read when you're angry. But it's true. Thinking of ways to get revenge only hurts *us,* because we're dwelling on it. But when we let go of our anger, we're free of it.

Pest Control

When have you felt like a pesky insect? What did you do about it?

Have you ever treated anyone else like a pest? Describe the situation.

Ask Christ to put his forgiveness in your heart toward those who have wronged you and to give you his love and understanding toward those you've wronged.

it takes guts

2 Corinthians 2:5,7-8

Remember Robert, Jeffrey, and Daniel? Well, Robert stayed angry for over a week at Jeffrey. After all, it was pretty mean of Jeffrey to ignore him all night and spend time with Daniel (who wasn't supposed to be invited anyway).

Jeffrey acted normal around Robert, and that made Robert even angrier. Finally, he'd had it with Jeffrey. Jeffrey had to know that he had hurt him. Robert decided to talk with him. The problem was getting him alone. A popular guy, Jeffrey always had a crowd around him. Robert finally caught up with him after fifth period.

"Hey, man, I need to talk with you," Robert said hesitantly.

"Sure! Do you want to grab the bench after school? I've got half an hour before I have to be at practice," Jeffrey said.

As soon as the end-of-the-day bell rang, Robert leaped out of his seat. This thing was bugging him, and he wanted it resolved. Robert told Jeffrey how he'd felt that night and how he was feeling now. Jeffrey was astounded. "I didn't know you felt like that, Robert! I just thought it would be nice to invite Daniel since he was new at school and all. I didn't know it would hurt your feelings."

After they talked, Robert felt relieved. Jeffrey liked him and was really a nice guy after all!

Fairy-Tale Ending?

Maybe you're thinking, *That's a fairy-tale ending. No guy would react like that.* Sure, not all endings to problems work out that easily, but we at least have to try. It *can* happen that way.

Christ holds us responsible to live in harmony with others. As Christians, we're to be role models, displaying the Lord to others.

I Just Can't!

Maybe you're saying, "But I've really been hurt. You don't understand how I feel or you couldn't ask me to go to that jerk!" Maybe someone has backbitten you, blabbed something he or she shouldn't have, or made up a lie about you. But Christ still holds you responsible to go to that person. He wants no division between his children. God wants us to be at peace in our relationships. Through the apostle Paul's words God calls us to live this way:

> If anyone has caused grief, he has not so much grieved
> me as he has grieved all of you [in the church].... Now
> instead, you ought to forgive and comfort him, so that
> he will not be overwhelmed by excessive sorrow. I
> urge you, therefore, to reaffirm your love for him.
> (2 Corinthians 2:5,7-8)

If you feel or cause sorrow, Christ also feels it. And the rest of the body of Christ feels it because we are all parts of one unified body.

I Can

 Confronting someone takes guts. Whether we are the ones who have been hurt or the ones who have done the hurting, God can give us the power to take the first step. Is there someone you should approach today? Write the name here and then list some positive qualities about this person (even if it's tough to do right now).

When you talk with the person you've just named, first share the good qualities you appreciate about him or her. People are more willing to listen if you compliment them first before presenting the problem.

Paul said in Philippians 4:13, "I can do everything through him who gives me strength." Christ was the one who gave Paul strength. Ask Christ to help you swallow your ego and to give you courage.

when you mess up

Psalm 103:2-4

Kathy sank into the leather couch. *Everything is such a mess! And it's all my fault!* She knew that no one else could get her out of what she had done. This one topped the charts.

Erika had been at Churchill High for six weeks after moving there from California. As far as Kathy knew, she was an only child. Since Kathy and Erika both played flute in band, they struck up a friendship. After spending lots of time with Kathy, Erika had dropped a bombshell.

Erika and Kathy had been munching peanut-butter cookies in the kitchen. Then Erika said, "Can I tell you something? Can you keep a secret?"

Kathy felt privileged that Erika wanted to tell her a secret. "Sure," she said without giving it a second thought.

"Well, there's something I've been wanting to tell you for a long time. You see, I do have a brother...back in California. He's nine years older than me and..." Her voice dropped to a whisper. "Well, he's gay, and he lives with another guy." Kathy was shocked. Rumors went around that some of the kids at school were gay, but she couldn't imagine what it would be like to have a *brother* who was gay.

A couple of weeks later at school, Kathy and some of her friends were talking. Somehow they got on the subject of gay people. Before Kathy realized it, Erika's secret had slipped out of her lips. It didn't take long to get around school, and the kids started to make fun of Erika. Kathy felt responsible—and she was.

When There's No Eraser

Kathy's stuck in an awful position. After ruining someone's life and reputation, there's not much she can do to repair it. It's like poking someone's eye out; there's nothing you can do to make that eye grow back. Kathy can't erase that news from the minds or memories of the kids at Churchill High. She's miserable.

Backspace

Kathy can't change the circumstances, but she does need to confess her sin. Scripture assures us that confession leads to forgiveness by God:

> If we confess our sins, he is faithful and just and will forgive us our sins and purify us from all unrighteousness. (1 John 1:9)

Confessing our sins to God is like typing the backspace key on a computer keyboard, deleting what came before. Our sins are gone forever from God's file. But we must do more than just confess our sins to God.

Not only must Kathy confess her sin to God and say she's sorry, but in addition she must take action. First she must admit to Erika that what she did was wrong and that she's very sorry. Then she must ask Erika to forgive her. Finally she must forgive herself (which is perhaps the hardest of the three things to do). We'll talk more about these steps in the upcoming days.

Wiping Up the Mess

Kathy can't change what happened, but she can change her reaction to it. She can mope around and say, "I'm such a loser." Or she can realize she's made a mistake and do what she can to make it right with Erika by defending her in front of the other students.

Have you ever made a mess of something? What was it?

If you've hurt someone else, contact that person. If he or she won't talk with you, leave a note on his or her locker. Or bake something to show you care about the other person's hurt. Read David's psalm for encouragement today:

Praise the LORD, O my soul,
  and forget not all his benefits—
who forgives all your sins,
  and heals all your diseases,
who redeems your life from the pit
  and crowns you with love and compassion.
    (Psalm 103:2-4)

healing the wound—for good

Romans 14:19

Again we meet Kathy and Erika. But this time, let's look at Erika's side.

Erika was embarrassed and upset when all the kids started poking fun at her, saying things like, "If your brother's gay, are you a lesbian?" Then they'd skitter off down the hall, laughing.

But what really crushed her was that she'd trusted Kathy with her deepest secret. How could Kathy have told anyone? Kathy tried to talk to her at school, but Erika just ignored her and walked on by. And when Kathy e-mailed her, Erika deleted the messages without reading them. Finally, though, a month later, Erika was so lonely that she agreed to hear what Kathy had to say—by phone.

Kathy poured out her story in tears and said how sorry she was. Up till now, Erika had seen her as an enemy. Suddenly she seemed human—she hurt just like Erika.

But still Erika couldn't forgive her. Kathy had ruined her life, and she could never trust her again. So after mumbling on the line, "I'm sorry, I really don't want to talk with you," Erika hung up.

Seventy Times Seven

Forgiveness is really hard to give, especially when it's *your* neck in the noose. It's even harder when the person who fails you was someone you trusted.

When Peter asked Jesus, "Lord, how many times shall I forgive my brother when he sins against me? Up to seven times?" (Matthew 18:21), Peter thought he was being saintly and generous. He was shocked at Jesus' response: "Seventy times seven." It blew him away.

Scar Tissue

Ending a conflict is as hard as keeping New Year's resolutions. Old scars keep showing up red at the surface. But Scripture challenges us:

> Let us…make every effort to do what leads to peace
> and to mutual edification. (Romans 14:19)

And the writer of Hebrews encouraged us with the way God forgives:

> I will forgive their wickedness
> and will remember their sins no more.
> (Hebrews 8:12)

Our task is pretty clear: to forgive and forget. Two very simple but difficult words.

A Superhuman Dose

Do you need to forgive someone? Why?

In your prayer time today, ask for God's forgiveness. Ask him to help you forgive yourself. Then contact the person you're having problems with. Be sincere and honest. Whether he or she accepts your efforts or not, you'll know you've obeyed God. And you can commit the rest of the process to him.

are old people really human?

Jeremiah 1:7-8

Tia leaned back against the sofa cushions and sniffed her steaming hot chocolate. "This is such a wonderful place," she sighed, snuggling into the creamy afghan. Coming here once a week was always worth the five-block walk, even in the middle of winter.

Martha (that's what Mrs. Maggiori had asked Tia to call her) was a terrific lady, even if she was Tia's English teacher. She seemed to care a lot about the kids she taught, more so than the average teacher.

One day early in the school year, when Tia was feeling down, Martha had noticed and had invited her over to her house after school. Martha thought of everything, even calling Tia's mom so she wouldn't be worried. During their talk, Tia discovered that Martha's husband had died a year ago and that she was lonely.

At first Tia visited Martha once a week because...well, she felt sorry for her. But by December things had changed drastically. Tia looked forward to their time together. Martha was the first older woman she *wanted* to spend time with. Martha giggled over Tia's jokes, loved chocolate (especially gooey, half-baked brownies—Tia's favorite), and comforted her when she'd had a bad day.

For the first time in her life, Tia had a true friend she could share with—the good things as well as the bad. Martha understood. Tia only wished that they'd found each other earlier.

Family Friends

Believe it or not, Tia and Martha aren't the only people in the history of the world to have an unusual relationship like that. Ruth and Naomi, the central figures in the Bible's book of Ruth, are another shining example. Naomi was Ruth's mother-in-law, but the old stereotype of the mother-in-law not getting along with the wife didn't apply here. Even as family members, they had an incredible friendship.

When Ruth's husband died, Ruth didn't leave Naomi to remarry. Naomi was a widow too, and Ruth stayed to be a loving support because the older woman was alone. This was unusual because, outside of marriage, women had no secure place in that culture and they usually remarried. Because of her love for Naomi, Ruth endured being an outsider who had no protection from a husband.

God blessed Ruth for her friendship with the older woman. He gave her a wonderful home and husband and blessed Naomi with grandchildren in her old age. Eventually, King David would be Ruth's great-grandson!

Disciple Making

The apostle Paul had an unusual relationship with Timothy, who he called "my beloved son." From reading the New Testament, we can gather the following information about Timothy: He was a young man, somewhat timid, and not physically well. Although they were miles away from each other, Paul wrote him the two biblical letters known as 1 and 2 Timothy, encouraging him to stand strong in his faith and to rekindle his desire to serve God.

Bridging the Gap

Be friends with an older person? "You've got to be kidding," you might say. "I have nothing in common with old people, and besides, they wouldn't understand me. Everybody knows there's a big gap between adults and teens."

Perhaps there really is a gap between *some* teens and *some* adults. But who says there has to be? There are lots of things teens can learn from older people. Solomon, the world's wisest man, encouraged young people this way:

> Listen to advice and accept instruction,
>   and in the end you will be wise. (Proverbs 19:20)

And—surprise!—there are many wonderful things adults can learn from teens, such as a renewed zest for life, a different vocabulary, and some ideas for creative fun. Just think what a terrific relationship you and an older person may be missing!

Write down the name of an older person you could pursue a friendship with. (If you can't think of any, ask your pastor to connect you with some of the older adults at your church. Or try visiting a senior center, a retirement facility, or a nursing home. You'll be surprised what spunky older people you find there!)

 List several activities you could do with this older person. (It could be watching a video, cooking dinner together, looking over scrapbooks or photo albums, playing miniature golf, or something else. The list is endless!) Give yourself one week to carry out your plan.

If the idea of getting together with an older person scares you, here's some encouragement from the book of Jeremiah:

> "Do not say, 'I am only a child.' You must go to every-
> one I send you to and say whatever I command you. Do
> not be afraid of them, for I am with you and will rescue
> you," declares the LORD. (1:7-8)

hopscotch is kid stuff

Matthew 18:3-5

"Rebecca, I'm over here!" Michael called and ducked behind the sofa in the Children's Care Center. Rebecca chortled and scampered in his direction as quickly as her chubby five-year-old legs could carry her.

The change in this little girl was incredible. Just two weeks ago, Rebecca had been abandoned on the steps of the center where Michael worked after school. At first she just rocked on the floor with her fists clenched tightly in her lap. She would sit like that with her head down for hours.

Then one day Rebecca surprised Michael by climbing into his lap. She looked at him, her blue eyes large with unspoken questions until he hugged her.

After that day, Michael and Rebecca were buddies. Michael spent even more volunteer time than usual at the center. Somehow he surprised himself: *I can't believe it. I really care about these kids!*

His work was no longer just a job.

Number One in God's Eyes

It's easy to think that children are just little rug rats, curtain climbers, things that get in our way and under our feet. But Jesus loved children and thought highly of them.

When some children were brought to Jesus so he could pray for them, the disciples rebuked them and were going to send them away. But Jesus said, "Let the little children come to me, and do not hinder them, for the kingdom of heaven belongs to such as these" (Matthew 19:14). Jesus didn't think that children were bothersome; he took time to love them and pray for them.

Who's the Greatest?

When Jesus talked affectionately with his disciples, he called them "children." And he gave them a big lesson about faith. When the disciples gathered around Jesus, asking who would be greatest in the kingdom of heaven, Jesus brought a child before them and said:

> I tell you the truth, unless you change and become like little children, you will never enter the kingdom of heaven. Therefore, whoever humbles himself like this child is the greatest in the kingdom of heaven.
>
> And whoever welcomes a little child like this in my name welcomes me. (Matthew 18:3-5)

By now, the disciples' mouths were hanging open in shock. A kid—the greatest? In those days children were seen but not heard; they had no rights. So Jesus' teaching stunned the disciples. But they were even more astonished when Jesus continued to say that children were so important that it would be better for someone to be drowned than to cause a little child to sin!

Focus on Kids

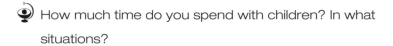 How much time do you spend with children? In what situations?

Is the time you spend with children voluntary or something you feel you have to do? For instance, do you go to your five-year-old cousin's birthday party just because your mom is making you? Do you baby-sit just to get extra cash when underneath it all you *hate* kids?

The next time you're with children, whether it's your choice or not, use your time to shine as a light for God. Remember, what you say and do is extremely important to a child because he or she will look up to you as a role model. Ask God to give you a loving heart toward those kids around you.

more than a brother

Ephesians 4:1-3

It was 4:00 A.M. Erin paced back and forth in front of the bay window. Every two minutes, she parted the curtains and peered out into the rainy blackness.

"Where is he? He should be here by now!" she said out loud, though no one else was in the room.

It was Friday night—no, early Saturday morning—and Erin was worried about her brother Joel. He was never late for anything. Because it was Erin's sixteenth birthday tomorrow, he was coming from Rockville College to celebrate with her. And he'd promised her a ride in the red Miata he'd just bought from another guy at college.

Erin had tried to fall asleep on the couch, but she just couldn't, except for short snatches. Every time she heard voices or the slamming of a car door, she woke up with a start. But by 4:00, she was wide awake. Visions of all the horrible things that might have happened to him flew through her mind. Maybe he'd stopped to get gas and someone had stolen his car. Or—even more horrible—maybe he'd fallen asleep at the wheel and crashed!

Erin thought back to the times when, as kids, they'd fought over toys and bicycles. She recalled the snotty comments she had made when he started shaving and wearing cologne. And then there was the time in fifth grade when she got really mad and bit him because he read her diary!

Still, in spite of their fights, Joel was a great brother. He really stuck up for her. *Kind of like a guardian angel,* Erin thought. Tears flooded her eyes.

Just then she heard a car door slam and feet tripped up the stairs. *Joel!* Erin flung the door open and threw herself in her brother's arms.

For the first time in her life she realized that her brother was not just her brother—he was her friend.

Getting Along

Getting along isn't easy, especially when it's with someone you have to be around all the time, like a member of your family. Maybe it's that pesky younger brother who's always nagging you to fly kites with him (and you think that would be terribly uncool). Or perhaps your younger sister gets into everything, including your makeup, clothes, and personal journal. Or maybe your older brother does geeky things that embarrass you.

Somehow it's hard for that "brotherly love in Christ" kind of feeling to stretch to your own relatives. Maybe you even wish that you had been born into a different family because your own is so weird!

Relative Power

The Bible gives us examples of people who were siblings and actually got along. Sure, it wasn't always easy, but they worked at their relationships.

Martha, Mary, and Lazarus are one such example. Martha and Mary were as different as any two people could be. Martha ran her legs off, trying to be the perfect hostess when Jesus came over for a visit. Mary, on the other hand, wanted to spend time with Jesus, so she hung around, right by his feet. And the result? Martha got mad at Mary, called her a lazy bum, and complained to Jesus about it (see Luke 10:38-42). Undoubtedly, that wasn't the only sisterly incident like that.

But even though Martha and Mary had lots of differences to work through, they shared two common loves—their brother Lazarus and Jesus Christ. When Lazarus died, they both mourned his death and begged Jesus to heal him (see John 11). What a family celebration there must have been when Lazarus walked out of his tomb with the grave clothes streaming from him!

Take Your Home's Temperature

First John 3:10 warns,

> This is how we know who the children of God are and
> who the children of the devil are: Anyone who does not
> do what is right is not a child of God; nor is anyone
> who does not love his brother.

In short, God is saying that anyone who does not love his brother or sister—and that includes actual brothers and sisters, our siblings—is not his child. Christ calls us to treat our family members with love and respect, and he wants us to keep harmony in our homes.

How do you treat your family members? Make notes about your individual relationship with each one of them.

Is there a family member you're having problems with? If so, jot down some ideas about how you can make peace with him or her.

During your prayer time today, read the following verses. Then ask God to help you live them out:

> Live a life worthy of the calling you have received. Be completely humble and gentle; be patient, bearing with one another in love. Make every effort to keep the unity of the Spirit through the bond of peace. (Ephesians 4:1-3)

people who grow on you—like fungus

James 2:1-4,8-9

For weeks, Trent, the number-one geek of the school, had been following Lauren around the school halls. No matter where she was—class, her locker, right outside the girls' restroom—he showed up. So far, Lauren had been pretty good at avoiding him. But today her luck had run out.

I can't believe it! Lauren thought. *He's such a lame-o! And why does he have to sit at my lunch table?* Carefully she lowered her orange tray with her milk and hamburger lunch special to the opposite end of the table. With a quick smile, she nodded to him and eased into the attachable bench seat.

I'm so glad Mary and Susan are on their way. Phew! Lauren sighed. But her relief was short-lived. In one clumsy act, Trent scooped up his tray and swooped down next to her.

Oh no! This is so-o-o embarrassing! Lauren screamed inside. *I'd rather kiss my brother than sit next to this guy!* Her stomach flip-flopped. This was the worst day of her life.

Unlovable People

If you were Lauren, what would you do? Loving or even liking "unlovable" people is tough, especially when you feel like your popularity is on the line. After all, why should you put yourself out for a goof or a geek, right? They can take care of themselves.

Jesus had to deal with unlovables. And even though he was perfect and sinless, he probably didn't always find it easy. So he can identify with you, whether it's the girl in your math class who never washes her hair or the smelly guy whose locker is next to yours (sometimes you might feel like putting a can of deodorant in his locker when he's not looking).

Playing Favorites

The book of James talks a lot about attitudes and playing favorites:

> My dear brothers and sisters, how can you claim that
> you have faith in our glorious Lord Jesus Christ if you
> favor some people more than others?
>
> For instance, suppose someone comes into your
> meeting dressed in fancy clothes and expensive jewelry,
> and another comes in who is poor and dressed in shabby
> clothes. If you give special attention and a good seat to
> the rich person,…doesn't this discrimination show that
> you are guided by wrong motives?…
>
> Yes indeed, it is good when you truly obey our
> Lord's royal command found in the Scriptures: "Love
> your neighbor as yourself." But if you pay special atten-

tion to the rich, you are committing a sin, for you are
guilty of breaking that law. (2:1-4,8-9, NLT)

Turning Garbage to Good

When Jesus met an adulterous woman (see John 8:1-11), he didn't roll his
eyes and dump her like some soggy, smelly piece of garbage. Boldly, he
listened to her problems. And finally he comforted her and gave her a new
chance at life. He took her immoral, "garbagy" life and made it beautiful
and clean.

Your Chance

Are there any people in your school who bug you? Who are
they, and why do you see them that way?

What difference would it make in your attitudes and actions if
you saw them as people whom God loves and then started
treating them that way?

What can you do this week to extend Jesus' love to the "unlovables" in your school? Make it simple and practical (it could be writing them a note, eating lunch with them, or even sharing a friendly "hello").

Remember to ask yourself, *Am I treating these people as Jesus would?*

sharks or non-christians?

Romans 8:37

Kimberly darted past David with a quick "hi" and hurriedly rounded the corner into her homeroom. Gratefully, she sank onto the chair and plopped her books on the floor.

Whew! I just got out of that one! She sighed deeply. She was so glad this was the end of the school year. And yet she was sad, too—she liked David as a person. But lately things had been taking an unexpected turn; she felt something more for him.

Just then she heard a shuffling sound. There he was. David—Mr. Detective. "Hey, Kimberly. I'm really interested in this God stuff. Maybe I could go to your Bible study with you sometime?" David asked.

"Uh, yeah. That would be good," Kimberly blurted out. "But tonight's the last Bible study until fall."

"Great! I'll come tonight. I can even pick you up, okay?" Reluctantly, Kimberly agreed. After tonight, he'd think she was a religious freak, and he'd never want to talk with her again.

Which Do You Fear the Most?

Sharks or non-Christians? When a non-Christian approaches you, do you immediately scramble out of the water or do you gulp and wait for the big bite? But are non-Christians really as deadly as they appear? Will they warp you and make you forget your Christianity, or worse yet, laugh at you? Maybe you're afraid you'd have to become their personal prayer warrior and pray them into getting saved. Or maybe you're worried that talking to them is a waste of time.

Even worse, like Kimberly, maybe you're attracted to that person and would love to go out on a date with him or her. *Would it really be so bad to date that cute guy?* you wonder. *He seems nice enough.*

DANGER—Beware

Christ calls us to go into all the world and share the good news. That means sharing it through your life, such as with your words and actions to your biology lab partner. But God also warns us about the kinds of relationships we should *not* have with non-Christians.

Paul tells us that marrying non-Christians is out (see 2 Corinthians 6:14). But what about *dating* non-Christians?

The Bible doesn't state in black and white that you should not date an unbeliever, but it *does* give directing principles. It talks about how the heart gets involved in relationships. And once you have that type of involvement, there's a lot of hurt in breaking it off—for both of you. Remember, the purpose of dating is not only to have fun and get to know more about others and yourself; it's also to point you toward a possible marriage partner.

Second Corinthians 6:14 makes it clear:

> Don't team up with those who are unbelievers. How
> can goodness be a partner with wickedness? How can
> light live with darkness? (NLT)

Jesus—1; Sharks—0

When Jesus died on the cross, he triumphed over Satan. He is only await-
ing the final victory. And because we are his children, we can claim his
power, even in relating to non-Christians:

> We are more than conquerors through him who loved
> us. (Romans 8:37)

> Do not be afraid or discouraged because of this vast
> army. For the battle is not yours, but God's. (2 Chron-
> icles 20:15)

So the battle is already won! All we have to do is show up every day for
service, knowing that Christ has already triumphed. What could be better?

What kinds of relationships do you have with non-Christians?

What could you do to draw a non-Christian friend closer to God?

What do you need to steer clear of in your relationships with non-Christians, especially those of the opposite sex?

In your prayer time, thank God that, through Christ, he has already won our spiritual battle. Rejoice that he already has a death grip on Satan's neck. Ask him for courage to share your faith and to hold tightly to *his* principles for godly relationships.

best-friend-of-the-year award

Deuteronomy 31:8

Laura and Bridget did everything together, like band and drama club and going out on weekends. When Laura's boyfriend dumped her, Bridget was there. And Bridget and Laura cried together when Bridget's brother died in a car accident. They were two parts of the same heart; each could tell when the other was hurting. And they could talk about anything, no matter how personal or embarrassing it was. They had perfect trust in each other.

Then Bridget's family moved when her dad, who was an Army colonel, got transferred to Germany. Bridget and Laura cried together for a week. And then suddenly, Bridget was gone. Laura clung to the photos of the two of them together and to the stuffed raccoon that Bridget had left her. But the empty feeling remained. How she wished Bridget were here! She was so lonely.

It's not fair, God! Laura cried out. *She was my best friend in the whole world. I'll never find someone else like her!*

Months later, Laura's heart still ached for her best friend.

Friends with God?

We've all lost friends at one time or another. But there's one friend who will *never* leave us, who is continually there, and who stands by our side no matter what. Who is this Super Friend? God.

Maybe you're saying to yourself, You've got to be kidding! No one can be friends with God. God's the guy who grabs a big stick and whacks you if you're not good. And besides, you can't touch someone who doesn't have a body.

If you're wondering what kind of "person" God really is, the best way to find out is to read the Bible. Think of it as a camera that takes God's photograph.

Focus on God

What makes God a good friend? He has all the qualities (and many, many more) of great friends that we've studied in this book—love, loyalty, a listening ear. But unlike human friends, God is always there. Check out these verses for starters:

> Do not be afraid or discouraged, for the LORD is the one
> who goes before you. He will be with you; he will neither
> fail you nor forsake you. (Deuteronomy 31:8, NLT)

> I still belong to you;
>   you are holding my right hand.
> You will keep on guiding me with your counsel,
>   leading me to a glorious destiny. (Psalm 73:23-24, NLT)

God has said,

    "I will never fail you.

        I will never forsake you."

That is why we can say with confidence,

    "The LORD is my helper,

        so I will not be afraid.

    What can mere mortals do to me?"

        (Hebrews 13:5-6, NLT)

Why not do your own search through Scripture to find out more about the kind of person God is?

Never Too Busy

Jesus is the best listener anyone could ever have. And he can be yours. In fact, he's listening right now for you to tell him your needs and desires. And the best thing of all is that his cell phone's always on. You'll never be sent to voice mail. And there are no roaming charges.

How do *you* picture God? Write down some of his qualities.

Do you see God as a friend and great listener or as somebody who whacks you if you're not good? Why?

If you were getting to know someone, how would you accomplish that?
Well, you'd probably talk with him or her—and then listen to what that
person says. In your prayer time today, ask God to show you what kind of
friend he really is. Get to know him better through talking with him and
reading his words in the Bible.

somebody you can't shock

1 Peter 5:7,10

Just when everything was starting to go great again, John felt like quitting. After two years, he'd finally become interested in life again. A counselor had helped him climb out of the depression that had seemed to bury him.

He knew the peaceful, happy feeling was too good to last. Now it was happening all over again. He couldn't talk with his parents—they didn't pay much attention to him anymore. As far as they were concerned, John was "out of danger." They were sure he wouldn't embarrass them by trying to kill himself again.

John had met his buddy Steven at a volleyball game last summer. Steven was a cool guy, and he took a special interest in John. This year, when John found out they'd be going to the same school, he was thrilled. He'd finally found a friend.

Or at least he'd thought so. Last week he'd shared his secret with Steven—the secret about how he had tried to commit suicide. Steven had looked at him as if he were some kind of freak. But Steven had promised he wouldn't tell anyone.

Within days, though, Steven had let the secret slip to a couple of guys.

Now they were all being so nice that it was getting on John's nerves. He didn't want to feel like someone's "ministry."

Who Can You Trust?

John found out the hard way that not everyone can be trusted. He was bummed. He wondered if there was *anyone* in the world who could be trusted with the way he really felt and what he thought about.

Sometime in our lives, all of us have felt like John did. For you, maybe it was when your best friend told a secret about you. Or when you found out the *real* reason that popular guy asked you out (it was on a dare called "Ask-the-Ugly-Out Night"). You were humiliated.

God Is Up-Front and Unshockable

Have you ever wished there were someone who knew you—and loved you anyway? Someone who is never shocked? Someone who knows about the lies you told, the CD you stole from the store, or the gossip you passed on about a classmate at school? Somebody who knows your parents are having a tough time right now? We do have somebody like that—God. And Scripture proves it:

> Cast all your anxiety on him because he cares for
> you....
>
>   And the God of all grace, who called you to his eternal glory in Christ, after you have suffered a little while, will himself restore you and make you strong, firm and steadfast. (1 Peter 5:7,10)

As you open yourself up to God's love, you'll find new hope. Jesus accepts you just as you are. He understands your joys and hurts completely, even when others don't.

Open Hands

 How do you feel about the fact that God knows you intimately?

Try doing this exercise during your prayer time: Write down anything that's bothering you today on a piece of paper. Crunch that paper into a ball in your fist. Then turn your palm up, holding the wad of paper over a wastebasket. Lift up your concerns to God in prayer, then when you're done praying, turn your hand upside down and let the paper fall in the wastebasket.

That's how we can treat the things that are bothering us when we believe God cares about us and has control of everything in our lives. The Bible tells us, "If the Holy Spirit controls your mind, there is life and peace" (Romans 8:6, NLT). That's a great reward for giving up your concerns to God!

playing games

John 15:13-14

"Benjamin!" Benjamin turned just in time to see Patrick dashing across his front lawn. "Dude, I'm glad I caught you. Do you want to go to a concert with me tomorrow? My brother won free tickets on the radio, but his girlfriend wants him to do something else tomorrow night," Patrick wheezed, out of breath from his run.

"Sure, I'll go if you help me mow the lawn today. I promised I'd do it," Benjamin replied. Patrick's fist tightened. He liked Benjamin a lot, but sometimes Benjamin got to him. Benjamin always put conditions on everything so other people would help him out with his work. Still, Patrick really wanted to go to the concert with Benjamin, so he agreed. They got the lawn done in a couple of hours.

The next night, Patrick stopped over at Benjamin's house to pick him up for the concert. He was surprised to see Benjamin lounging around in his sweats, playing a video game.

"Oh!" Benjamin called out. "I didn't know that the concert was tonight. Sorry! I can't go; I have to baby-sit my little sister. Some other time."

Patrick stormed out the door, furious. It was Benjamin's typical game. As soon as someone else helped him do his work, he canceled out on doing what they wanted to do. Patrick had had it up to his ears with him. That was Benjamin's last chance, and he'd blown it.

Are Your Friends Conditional?

Has anyone ever played the "condition" game with you? Things like "I'll help you with your term paper if you'll come to my party tomorrow" or "I'll like you if you get your hair cut the way I think you should" or "You have to buy the hippest clothes if you want to be a member of our crowd." How does that make you feel? Usually downright mad. Maybe, like Patrick, you feel used. Or maybe you feel that people are just looking at your outside and not at the inside. They want you to conform to being who *they* want you to be, not who you really are.

God's Condition

Unlike humans, God puts only one condition on his friendship with you—that you accept him into your life unconditionally. He wants to come in and transform you into the best person you can be. He won't play popularity games with you. You're either totally his or you belong to Satan. There's no living in-between the two.

God loved us so much that he sent his Son, Jesus, to take all our sins on himself. Jesus died in agony on the cross, nails piercing his hands and feet. But he did it out of love and compassion for each one of us. Jesus gave his life because he created us and loves us immensely.

> The greatest love is shown when people lay down their
> lives for their friends. You are my friends if you obey
> me. (John 15:13-14, NLT)

But the problem is that we've all sinned against God (see Romans 3:23)—we want to do everything our own way. We deserve punishment, and yet Christ took it for us.

What's our part? We need to make some choices: believe that Christ died for us, tell him that we're sorry for our sin and that we want to be changed, and invite Jesus to be our Forever Friend and Savior for the rest of our lives. And then we will have the best unconditional Friend and Life Transformer anyone could ever have!

True Blue

Accepting Jesus as your Friend and Savior, your Guard and Guide, is the only condition to having him as your number-one, true-blue Friend who will never leave you.

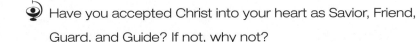 Have you accepted Christ into your heart as Savior, Friend, Guard, and Guide? If not, why not?

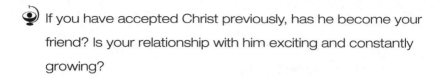 If you have accepted Christ previously, has he become your friend? Is your relationship with him exciting and constantly growing?

Christ longs for a close relationship with you. His one condition is that you accept him wholeheartedly as your number-one priority. Ask God to help make you willing to discover more about him. Make these verses your prayer:

> I pray…that the eyes of your heart may be enlightened in order that you may know the hope to which he has called you, the riches of his glorious inheritance in the saints, and his incomparably great power for us who believe. (Ephesians 1:18-19)

the forever friend

Romans 14:7-8

Brandon's heart ached. He couldn't believe it could hurt so much, even after five years.

Last weekend he'd been invited to a barbecue with his friend Chaka's family. He had watched them all work together to get lunch ready—they were having so much fun. Brandon wished he had a dad. But his dad had left when Brandon was ten, and he could hardly even remember what his dad looked like. His mom had put away all the pictures in a locked drawer.

"Just once, God!" his soul cried out. "Why can't I have a dad like that—just for one day!"

Oddly enough, that Wednesday his youth group leader talked about how God is not only our Father (which Brandon had a hard time with because he thought fathers were bogus) but also our best friend. And even better, a Forever Friend who is always with us wherever we go.

Brandon hadn't prayed for a long time. Up till now, he really hadn't felt God cared much about him, or God wouldn't have let his dad leave. But tonight he prayed, "God, please be my dad. And God, be my

Forever Friend, too. I really need one. Amen." He felt happy for the first time in months.

Best Friends

If you've accepted Christ into your heart and life, you're his child. It's pretty wonderful to have a best friend and daddy all wrapped up in one. God is proud to call us his own:

> None of us lives to himself alone and none of us dies to himself alone. If we live, we live to the Lord; and if we die, we die to the Lord. So, whether we live or die, we belong to the Lord. (Romans 14:7-8)

The Power in You

When Jesus left earth and ascended to heaven, he didn't leave us alone to fend for ourselves. He sent the Holy Spirit to help us every day (see John 14:16-17).

God also gives us a huge promise:

> Do not fear, for I am with you;
>   do not be dismayed, for I am your God.
> I will strengthen you and help you;
>   I will uphold you with my righteous right hand.
>   (Isaiah 41:10)

The Best Is Yet to Come

God promises that the best is yet to come. Earth's like living in a garbage can compared to what's in heaven! And God is preparing a place in heaven for you. Just think—your very own room in the grandest mansion of all. But the best thing is that you'll be with your favorite Friend in a place where no tears will fall. Ever. That's *got* to be a fairy-tale ending.

 Jesus wants to be your Forever Friend. How can you draw closer to him this week?

Jesus is coming back at a time no one expects. What do you need to do to get your heart and mind ready to go with him?

Thank God today for the promises of his Word. Ask him to remind you constantly of his friendship and his love for you.

about the authors

Jeff and Ramona Tucker have over thirty years of combined ministry experience with middle-school and high-school students. Jeff is plant superintendent at a manufacturing facility. Ramona, former editor of *Today's Christian Woman* magazine, is now senior editor at Tyndale House Publishers. They and their daughter Kayla live in the Chicago area.

Hey, don't stop now.

If you really liked reading this devotional you may be interested to know that three more are available in the Red Hill Devos line. Written about you and for you, these books help you cope with life, friendships…maybe even long lines at the movies!

OTHER TITLES INCLUDE:

Someone Like Me: A Youth Devotional on Identity
    by Annette LaPlaca with foreword by Ash Mundae
This Thing Called Life: A Youth Devotional on Finding Direction
    by Jeff and Ramona Tucker with foreword by The Echoing Green
Forget Me Not: A Youth Devotional on Love and Dating
    by Mike Worley with foreword by Aurora

Real Devotions for Real Teens
from Shaw Books